Protecting The Rights Of THE ACCUSED IN NEW YORK

Michael A. Schillinger, Esq.

Jacobs & Whitehall
73-03 Bell Blvd, #10
Oakland Gardens, NY 11364
www.jacobsandwhitehall.com

Ordering Information:

Quantity sales. Special discounts are available on quantity purchases by corporations, associations, and others. For details, contact the publisher at the address above.

Orders by U.S. trade bookstores and wholesalers. Please contact Jacobs & Whitehall: Tel: (888) 991-2766 or visit www.jacobsandwhitehall.com.

Printed in the United States of America

Published in 2022

ISBN: 978-1-954506-57-2

DEDICATION

To my family, who have supported me and allowed me to pursue a career where I've been fortunate to touch so many lives.

Acknowledgements

I want to thank all of those that have stood beside me throughout my career. My family who has supported me every step of the way; my mentors who helped me develop my trial skills; my colleagues who are always there to advise me, and my clients who trust me and have allowed me to fight for their rights. I thank you all.

DISCLAIMER

This publication is intended to be used for educational and general informational purposes only. No legal advice is being given, and no attorney-client relationship is intended to be created by reading this material. The author assumes no liability for any errors or omissions or for how this book or its contents are used or interpreted, or for any consequences resulting directly or indirectly from the use of this book. Nothing in this publication should be taken as legal advice for any individual case or situation. Legal jurisdictions often differ on major and minor aspects of the law, and each legal situation is unique. Furthermore, the law frequently changes, and statutes are updated.

For legal or any other advice, please consult an experienced attorney or the appropriate expert, who is aware of the specific facts of your case and is knowledgeable in the law in your jurisdiction. While in some jurisdictions this publication may contain attorney advertising under applicable laws and ethical rules, prior results do not guarantee a similar outcome.

Law Office of Michael A. Schillinger, Esq.

www.michaelschillinger.com

(631) 650-6900

Forest Hills Office

118-21 Queens Blvd, Suite 518

Forest Hills, NY 11375

Long Island Office

142 Freeman Ave

Islip, NY 11751

Astoria Office

21-83 Steinway Street

Astoria, NY 11105

Testimonials

"I don't usually leave reviews for anything but Michael Schillinger is not only an attorney but a god sent Angel. He has been on top of my case from day one of calling him, he was always available to speak to me and was fast in responding to any concerns I had throughout the course of my case. He has eased so much anxiety and stress that we had as first time offenders who had no clue how the court system worked and he never once made us feel like we were being neglected. Michael was with us every step of the way and worked extremely hard to get us a deal leaving us with no criminal record or convictions. He is dedicated to his clients and truly does make sure you're well taken care of. His office even sent us a Christmas card for the holiday and that just touched my heart because of how much his office cares to go out of their way and little touches like that mean so much to people. I highly recommend Michael Schillinger with no doubts in my heart. You will not regret it! Thank you so much for everything you've done for my family and I, I am forever grateful to you.

-Cherry S

****

"Mr. Michael Schillinger is a very passionate and dedicated lawyer. He personally commits himself to his clients. When I hired him, he used his professional expertise of strong technical skill and super-critical thinking ability with in-depth legal research to build my defense. Anyone who hires Mr. Schillinger has a higher chance of a good result. Expect to receive a personal commitment and good representation from Michael Schillinger – a lawyer who sets his eyes on winning always!"

— James

****

"I 100% endorse Mike Schillinger. We worked together at the DA's Office for several years and he was by far one of the best attorneys at the Office. He's diligent, dedicated and very talented. If a family member or friend ever needed a criminal defense attorney, Mike Schillinger would be at the top of my list of recommendations. He will always zealously advocate for his clients and obtain the best result possible, whether it be a dismissal, a favorable plea deal or a victory after a hard fought trial."

— Luis, A Fellow Lawyer

****

"I am a financial services attorney from Washington, DC. A family member of mine recently contacted me regarding a criminal matter of hers in Suffolk County that had been outstanding for eight years. I found Michael based upon his strong reviews, as well as his experience as a former prosecutor. I am so happy that I contacted him. His calm and pleasant demeanor were a refreshing surprise. He handled my family member's case expertly. His cost estimates were highly accurate. He responded to every phone call and email the same day, often within minutes. He kept us apprised of all developments and concerns. He is a highly effective attorney and an excellent communicator. As an attorney myself, I recommend him without any reservation or qualification."

— John H.

****

"Michael is a Great Lawyer, Well-spoken and attentive. He made sure during every step of the process I was aware and understanding – whilst making sure everything was in my best. My case ended in a highly Favorable Decision due to his Dedication and Determination – I highly recommend !!"

— Branden

****

"Michael you are a very kind and understanding lawyer. You really want what's best for your clients. I would definitely recommend you to my family and friends. Thank you so much. A pleasure working with you."

— Christine S.

****

"Mike is an excellent attorney. He sat down with me and gave me all the time I needed. We were able to handle my issues that day. I would highly recommend him to anyone looking for a lawyer."

— Sean

****

TABLE OF CONTENTS

ABOUT THE AUTHOR

My name is Mike Schillinger and I'm a criminal defense attorney that practices in New York City and Long Island. I mainly practice Criminal Defense and Traffic Law, and I handle everything from traffic violations and misdemeanors, to serious violent felonies. My clients come from all walks of life, and I truly enjoy helping people through some of the most difficult periods of their lives.

I've always had a passion for helping people and have spent my entire career serving the public. In fact, while earning my Bachelor of Science degree in legal studies at St. John's University, I worked as a Congressional caseworker for a United States Congressman on Long Island. I spent about eight years in that position and handled all sorts of cases, including Immigration, Veteran's Affairs, IRS and tax issues, as well as many other types of federal cases. During that time, I had the privilege of helping people who had nowhere else to turn.

While still working for the Congressman, I continued my education at St. John's University School of Law. It was there that I realized my desire to help people extended to Criminal and Constitutional Law. I knew that I wanted to help protect the rights of my clients, to fight for them at trial, and to ensure that all their rights under the U.S. Constitution were upheld.

During law school, I also spent a lot of time participating in mock trials, mock litigation, and various tournaments throughout the country. While not a real trial, such "trial" practice prepared me for the real legal work I have done following law school. Some highlights of my participation in these tournaments included taking second place in New York State in the National Trial Lawyer's Competition, as well as second place in the American Bar Association Competition where I competed against schools from across the country.

Following law school, I took a position as an Assistant District Attorney at the Queens District Attorney's Office. There, I handled everything from violations and misdemeanors, all the way up to serious violent felonies. While I can't say exactly how many cases I handled as an ADA, I would probably say that the number ranges in the thousands, including gun cases, drug cases, serious violent felonies, sex offenses, and even some attempted murder cases, and kidnapping cases.

My time in the District Attorney's office led me to private practice, where I've continued handling all different case types, ranging from misdemeanors to felonies, including serious sex offenses, gun cases, and murder cases. Using the experience that I've gained over the course of my career, I fight for my clients and ensure that their rights are protected every step of the way. I make sure that everyone that walks through my door gets the advocacy that they need, the compassion that they want, and the dedication to their case that they deserve.

I find that most of my clients are otherwise good people who have made a mistake or are being wrongfully accused. Although most people look at someone who has been charged with a crime as a bad person, the fact is that this is simply not the case. We're all human beings and we all make mistakes. Because of that, when someone walks into my office, that's exactly how we treat them – humanly.

I know some attorneys tend to treat people as if they're just another number, another statistic, another file. That's not the case when you walk into my office. My strategy is to humanize my clients when presenting their cases to the District Attorney's Office. We'll discuss things like my client's background, where they're from, what their family is like, where they work, where they went to school, and how they are active in the community. I use this information when negotiating the case with the District Attorney's Office to help them understand that my clients are not just another file on their desk. I ensure that whenever I speak with the Assistant District Attorney on a case, they understand that my clients are real, genuine people in the community who have families, who work and contribute to our society, and who may have just made an error in judgment.

Knowing that a criminal charge is one of the most difficult situations my clients will face throughout their entire lives, I let each of them know - They are not alone. We will face and fight these charges together.

Former Assistant District Attorney

My background as a prosecutor gives me a unique perspective on the cases that come into my office. Sometimes people feel that I've "worked for the enemy," and yes that's true – I worked as an Assistant District Attorney. But that only serves to benefit my clients. My experience as a prosecutor helps me understand exactly what the other side is looking for.

This allows me to anticipate the plea deal, know what the ADA wants to see, and gives my clients an edge at the negotiation table. I'm also familiar with the alternative sentencing programs that many other lawyers simply don't know about. If it's a situation where we're talking about getting a client some sort of treatment, I'm familiar with the programs, with the community service process, the probation process and what options are available – and more importantly, I'm familiar with it from both sides of the aisle.

I also know how they're going to handle their case when they take it to trial - what weaknesses to look for and what to cross-examine the cops and witnesses on. As a former prosecutor, I've done direct examinations with countless cops, criminalists, breathalyzer techs, analysts – you name it. I know what to look for as if I were the prosecutor, giving me an edge in finding the weaknesses in their case, and the upper hand at trial.

Who Is This Book For?

I get a lot of people that come into my office telling me that their lawyer has not explained their case to them. They want to know what they should be doing while their case is pending, what certain things mean, and just generally what's going on with their case. I get a lot of people that come in and say, "Look, my attorney hasn't explained any of this to me. He/she hasn't even given me the paperwork and I'm really not sure what I'm facing." I am hoping that this book will help people understand a bit more about how a criminal case works, what they should expect and maybe fill in some of the gaps that other lawyers leave out. I want to help get those people the information that they need - the information that their lawyer should be explaining to them but may not be.

CHAPTER 1

THE ARREST – WHAT TO KNOW WHEN THE POLICE COME KNOCKING

Common Misconceptions

A good place to start is discussing some misconceptions that I find people have about being arrested and charged. Probably the most common misconception is that when someone is arrested, they think that everything is lost, and that there's nothing they can do to fix it. Just because you've been arrested does not mean that your life is over. It's not. You still have options.

As the case progresses, I explain to each of my clients that typically we will have numerous opportunities to try and resolve the case as favorably as possible. The first step in this process is the plea bargaining stage – this is when we sit down at the negotiating table with the District Attorney's Office.

If we're not able to come to a reasonable deal with the A.D.A., then the next tool in our tool-belt is motion practice. Depending on the facts of the case, there are many different motions we might file at this stage – for instance we may file a motion to suppress evidence on Constitutional grounds or otherwise demand suppression hearings, we may file a motion to preclude the D.A. from using evidence, or even to dismiss the case because the D.A. failed to meet their discovery or speedy trial burden. At any rate, after we file these motions, we generally end up at the next stage – the suppression hearings.

The specific facts of the case tend to dictate which types of suppression hearings will be conducted. These can include hearings to determine whether physical evidence, an identification procedure, or a statement should be suppressed, or even if there was no probable cause for the officer to arrest you in the first place.

Finally, if all else fails, we go to trial. Trial is our ultimate means of defense and that's where we're going to hold the District Attorney's Office to their burden – to prove the case beyond a reasonable doubt. We test their evidence, cross-examine their witnesses, present our own evidence, and fight like hell.

NEVER *Give A Statement To The Police*

When the police come knocking, do NOT give them a statement. I cannot say it enough – never give a statement to the police without speaking to an attorney first. Even if you think you're the most convincing person in the world, don't try talking yourself out of being arrested, it will not work. It's just not going to happen. It doesn't matter that your uncle is a cop, it doesn't matter that it didn't happen the way that the complainant said it happened. All that matters is whether or not the cop believes he has probable cause to arrest you. Once he determines that he is going to place you under arrest, regardless of anything that you say, he will arrest you and let the lawyers hash things out later. I'll say it again, if you're at risk of being arrested, do not give a statement to the police.

Now I have nothing but respect for law enforcement, and in fact my office has represented quite a few cops; but you must realize that they are not your friend in this situation. Their job is to arrest you and build a case against you. That includes getting you to confess. They must ensure that when they get the file over to the D.A., it has all of the evidence they will need to prosecute you. When you give them a statement, even if you think it helps your case, it typically just helps them. Sometimes, even saying something that you think is helpful, ends up only hurting you in the long run.

One thing that's important to understand is that the police can lie to you. In fact, it's a common tactic that they use when they're trying to get you to confess. They can tell you that if you just tell them what happened, everything will be okay - that they'll let you go home. Do not believe them – it's simply not the case. When you are their suspect, the police have one job to do, and that job is to arrest you.

If you are stopped by the police, the first words out of your mouth should be "I want to call my lawyer, I'm not speaking to you without him present." I tell every single one of my clients to carry my card in their wallet and to program my number into their phone. Always, always, always ask for a lawyer to be present during any conversation with law enforcement.

Do Not Consent To A Search

A common misconception that people have is that the cops are allowed to search their vehicle, person, bag, etc. That is simply not the case. In fact, you never have to consent to a search by the police. I'm not telling you that you should physically resist them – that is never a good idea. If you physically resist, you may end up with additional charges for resisting arrest and obstructing governmental administration, and you run the risk of the police officer responding with force and hurting you. Instead, what I mean is that you can let the officer know that you are not consenting to this search, and you can even ask to record the encounter.

If you consent to the search, you are giving up a Constitutional right without even knowing it. "But I have nothing to hide." Yes, that may be true. But are you 100% certain that there isn't a single item in your car or on your person that the cop can claim is illegal? What if your friend was in the back seat the day before and dropped drugs on the floor? What if you're borrowing someone's car and they have something illegal in it? What if you just didn't realize that the switchblade you bought out of state is illegal in New York? There is absolutely no benefit to consenting to a search by the police.

The bottom line is, when the cop asks you, "Is it okay if we search you? Is it okay if we search your car? Is it okay if we search your home?" Your answer is "No." Tell them no and let them do their job within the confines of the law and the Constitution. This allows your attorney to challenge the search throughout the course of your case, and can sometimes lead to evidence being suppressed and in certain circumstances, even a dismissal of the charges against you.

When Should I Contact A Criminal Defense Attorney?

You should contact a criminal defense attorney as soon as you even have a hint that you might be under investigation or under arrest. Contacting a criminal defense attorney early allows you to get ahead of the charges. In some cases, you might even be able to prevent being arrested at all.

Many people ask me, "Will I be able to contact an attorney when I'm being arrested?" I tell every one of my clients to put my number in their phone: [(631) 650-6900] and to carry my card in their wallet, just in case the officer does not allow them to use their personal cell phone. Then, if they're ever arrested, they can just tell the officer, "I want to contact my attorney," and he/she should let them reach out to me.

CHAPTER 2

HOW AND WHEN DO MIRANDA RIGHTS COME INTO PLAY?

Miranda rights - this is the thing that folks are probably most familiar with from TV. "You have the right to remain silent. Anything you say can and will be used against you in a court of law. You have the right to an attorney. If you cannot afford an attorney, one will be appointed for you." These are your Miranda warnings, and to answer one of the most common questions that I get, no, the police do NOT have to read you these every time that you are arrested.

The Miranda warning was created in 1966 as a result of the U.S. Supreme Court case *Miranda v. Arizona, 384 U.S. 436*. Their purpose is to protect people's Fifth Amendment right, which is the right to not answer self-incriminating questions.

That is the critical part – you have the right to not answer self-incriminating questions. This does not mean that the police cannot arrest you because they did not issue you *Miranda* warnings. What it means, is that under certain circumstances, if they take a statement from you without giving you *Miranda* warnings, that statement may be suppressible at an evidentiary hearing so that the District Attorney's Office cannot use it at trial against you.

However, you should understand that there are circumstances where the police can ask you questions without giving you *Miranda* warnings. One common example of this is when a cop arrives at the scene of an accident. They see your car has been involved in a motor vehicle accident, they walk up to you, and then they ask you some questions. They say something along the lines of, "Hey buddy. What happened here?"

If you turn around and say, "Well officer, I just drank a twelve pack and smashed into that guy's car," you are going to be hearing that statement at your arraignment, at your hearings, and eventually at your trial if your attorney can't resolve the inevitable DWI case that's going to result from that statement.

I'm sure your question is, why? He never read me my *Miranda* rights, why can't we suppress the statement like you said earlier? The reason a statement like that would not necessarily be suppressible, is because the officer was not engaged in "custodial interrogation." That is the key when we talk about suppressing statements based upon a *Miranda* violation.

For *Miranda* to come up, you must be in custody, and the officer must be interrogating you. What does it mean to be in custody? That's a question that often comes up at the suppression hearing (called a *Huntley* hearing in the New York State courts). The answer to that question is not as simple as you might think. It does not just mean that you're in handcuffs sitting in the back of a cop car. To determine custody, we typically ask whether a reasonable person in your situation, who has not committed any crime, would feel free to leave the presence of the cops.

When we start litigating the issue of whether you are in custody, many different things can come up. Were the cops physically holding you? Did they have weapons out? Were those weapons pointed at you? Did they tell you not to leave? How many officers were there? Were they in uniform? There are numerous questions that your attorney should ask you when preparing for a suppression hearing. Because of that, it's critical that you give your attorney as much information about the circumstances of your arrest from the beginning of your case.

The next question after we determine whether you were in custody or not, is were you subject to interrogation? Again – not as easy of a question as you might think – interrogation does not necessarily mean that you're sitting in a back room of a precinct with a bright light shining in your eyes, getting hit with a phone book. When we talk about interrogation, the conversation that you have with the police officer becomes crucial. How they asked you the questions, what they said, what you said – all these things come into play when we start trying to determine whether you were being interrogated.

Finally, if there was a custodial interrogation, then the question comes down to whether your statement was made voluntarily after knowingly waiving your *Miranda* rights. If the cop knows what he's doing, he's going to read you those rights, on video, and get an explicit answer from you as to whether or not you want to give a statement. When we talk about voluntariness, we look into whether there was any coercion, force, threats of force, whether you were intoxicated, and quite a few other factors. It may come up whether the questioning was simply investigatory, such as the example I gave above, but at any rate, these are some of the issues that your attorney should be going over with you when you sit down to prep for the suppression hearing on your case. With all of this being said, and this is something that I'm going to repeat a lot in this book – any time you encounter the police, the first words out of your mouth should always be "I want an attorney."

CHAPTER 3

WHAT HAPPENS IN THE FIRST 24 TO 72 HOURS OF AN ARREST?

The first 24 - 72 hours following an arrest are oftentimes the scariest. A good attorney will explain what to expect, and they should have an idea of how the arraignment process works in the county you're arrested in. The process can differ quite a bit depending on where you're arrested. I mostly practice in Queens, Suffolk and Nassau Counties, and will use these to illustrate some of the similarities and differences that can come up when you're charged with a crime.

Generally speaking, when you're arrested, you'll be brought back to the local precinct. The police will process you, do their paperwork and may even try to ask you some questions and interrogate you. They'll voucher the evidence, which basically means they seal it up in a secure envelope and send it over to the property clerk. At this stage – they're essentially focusing on getting the case ready for the District Attorney.

After that, you'll either be issued a desk appearance ticket, which is a slip of paper that's going to tell you that you have a future court date for your arraignment, or, depending on the allegations, you may instead be brought over to the Court for your arraignment.

Arrested In One Of The Five Boroughs

So, here's where we get into one of the differences. If you're in New York City and arrested in one of the five boroughs, the police are not going to write up the criminal court complaint. Instead, they'll be speaking with someone from the D.A.'s office (either an A.D.A. or a paralegal) who, with the officer's help, will draft up the complaint. The main way that this impacts you is that sometimes this can cause delays in the arrest to arraignment time for your case. During this time, they typically call the victim, they'll look at some of the body camera footage, and they'll review the evidence - essentially, they take all the steps necessary to get your file court-ready. Once these things are taken care of, they'll take you over to central bookings and to the courthouse to get you in front of the judge for your arraignment.

Arrested on Long Island

On Long Island it's a little bit different. The police handle most of the paperwork and write up everything themselves - this tends to result in less detailed complaints, but it can also result in faster processing of the complaint.

With that being said, one major difference to know about is if you're arrested on Long Island, depending on the time that you were arrested, you may not be transported to the Courthouse until the following day. In New York City, the police transport people to the courthouse all day/night until court closes - in Queens that's about 1:00 A.M.

On the other hand, in Suffolk County, if you're arrested after the bus has gone over to the courthouse, you're there until tomorrow. They generally transport to district court one time each day, so if you're not on that bus, you are likely going to end up waiting until the following day.

The Arraignment and Notices

It's all too often that I get a client walking into my office telling me that their attorney at the arraignment didn't explain anything to them. While this stage of the case happens very quickly, there's just no acceptable excuse that your lawyer can give for not explaining the arraignment process to you before you go out there.

The first thing to understand is that an arraignment is essentially a hearing. It may not seem like that because it's going to happen extremely quickly – but at the end of the day the arraignment is technically a hearing, and there's quite a few important things that are going to happen during it.

When we talk about being arraigned at the beginning of a case, it's going to happen one of two ways. Either you'll have gotten a desk appearance ticket and you'll walk into the courthouse on the return date, or, you'll have been held after being arrested, and you'll be brought out to see the judge from the holding cell. Either way, once you're in front of the Court, the first thing that will happen is the Assistant District Attorney will indicate that they've either filed a criminal court complaint or an indictment against you.

Then they're going to serve you with some notices. You're going to hear a bunch of numbers flying around that are going to be completely meaningless to you unless you've spoken with your attorney about them. I find that this is something that many attorneys forget to explain to their clients, so I'm including a brief explanation of the more common ones here:

- 710.30(1A) notice, commonly referred to as statement notice, is the District Attorney putting you on notice that they have a statement that you gave to law enforcement that they intend to use against you at trial.

- 710.30(1B) notice, commonly referred to as ID notice, is the District Attorney putting you on notice that they intend on using an identification procedure at trial. Essentially this means that someone picked you out of a photo array, show-up, or lineup procedure.
- 190.50 notice. This notice typically only comes up if you are charged with a felony. Essentially, it's the District Attorney putting you on notice that they intend on presenting your case to the Grand Jury for the purpose of indicting the case. This is a necessary step in felony cases and should not alarm you. The D.A. must give you this notice, because you have the right to testify in the Grand Jury on your own behalf, and therefore need to know when the Grand Jury will be hearing your case.
- 250.20 notice, commonly referred to as a demand for alibi, is the D.A. demanding that you give them notice if you intend on offering an alibi defense at trial.

After the Assistant District Attorney finishes serving his notices, your attorney may serve some notices on your behalf. Probably the most common defense notice is referred to as "Cross 190.50" Notice, or "Cross Grand-Jury" notice, and effectively means that you intend on testifying in the Grand Jury. Even if you don't necessarily know whether you're going to testify, it's important that your attorney preserves your right to testify so that you and he can discuss this at a later time.

Finally, one other thing to note, is that an arraignment doesn't only happen at the beginning of a case. Sometimes, typically in felony cases, after the Grand Jury has indicted you, you'll be arraigned again. The reason for this, is the indictment divests the criminal court of its jurisdiction over your case, and your case is then transferred to Supreme Court (or County Court if you're on Long Island).

The People Are Ready For Trial – What is Speedy Trial or CPL § 30.30?

You may then hear the A.D.A. say, "The people are ready for trial." This may happen at the arraignment, but nowadays with the new discovery laws it's more likely you'll hear it later in the case. When you hear it –

don't get alarmed. It doesn't mean that they're ready to actually start doing the trial today. That's not what they mean. It's effectively a term of art that stops the speedy trial or CPL § 30.30 clock.

I'm sure you're wondering, what is Speedy Trial? Speedy trial or 30.30 time, is the time period in which the District Attorney has to comply with their discovery obligations and to announce that they are ready to move your case to trial. I usually tell my clients to think about it like a stopwatch, because there are certain things that start the clock, and certain things that stop it. When you are initially arraigned, the speedy trial clock starts ticking. In certain situations, your attorney may advise you that "waiving speedy trial time" is in your best interest, because it signals to the District Attorney that you're reasonable, and that you're looking to resolve your case. While the District Attorney is legally not allowed to condition a plea agreement on a waiver of speedy trial, the reality of it is that by waiving speedy trial time, you give the A.D.A. assigned to your case additional time to investigate, and you give your attorney additional time to bring the A.D.A. around to your position.

A good example of this is when a client comes to me and tells me that they believe we will be able to obtain evidence that speaks to their innocence. Now on the one hand, we could wait for the District Attorney's Office and Police Department to conduct their investigation, and hope that they come across the video that proves your innocence. Doing that, however, opens us up to some risks. They may not find the evidence, they may not agree with our interpretation of it, or they may rush the case into the Grand Jury and indict it, leaving us now with a much bigger hurdle to overcome at the negotiation table.

Instead, sometimes what we do in cases like that, is we waive speedy trial time. We do that for two reasons – first, it stops the D.A. from rushing the case into the Grand Jury, leaving us open to more options when we sit down to negotiate. Second, it gives us time to get our ducks in a row and put together a packet of information to present to the District Attorney's Office on your behalf. This pre-pleading memorandum, or mitigation packet, will typically include character reference letters from your friends/family/colleagues, and it will also include evidence that we believe proves your innocence, as well as any legal research and caselaw that supports our position.

Order of Protection: Restraining Orders

The next thing that will happen at the arraignment is the A.D.A. may request an order of protection. I'll get into much more detail about orders of protection later, but generally speaking, an order of protection is what's more commonly known as a "restraining order." While ultimately the decision rests with the judge, when the order of protection comes up, your attorney's job is to advocate on your behalf with respect to the order. Depending on the circumstances, he may argue that the order shouldn't be issued at all, that a lesser or limited order of protection would be appropriate instead, or that there should be some sort of modification to the order, like an access order, marking the order subject to incidental contact, or marking it subject to family court modification.

This brings us to the thing that everyone is always dreading the most – bail.

Bail Requests

Bail in New York State, particularly after the new bail statute was put into place, is meant to ensure your return to court. It's not supposed to be punitive, it's not supposed to be based on the severity of the case, or the possibility that you might reoffend. It is an amount of money that the Court holds in an effort to ensure that you will make every single Court appearance, and abide by the Court's directives. If you don't, then that money can be forfeited, and you lose it.

With that being said, bail gets set in three different ways in New York State:

Cash Bail: Cash bail is typically going to be the lowest amount of bail that they're going to set, and it's exactly what it sounds like – it's an amount of cash that you (or a friend/family member) gives to the Court. It gets held and you get it back when the case is resolved, or it's forfeited if you end up warranting. In some circumstances you may be the one to post it, but, in most cases, your family or friends will typically post it on your behalf.

If you are the one who is posting bail for another person, you must be cautious. When you post bail for another person, you do so at your own risk. You are essentially assuring the Court that the person you're posting bail for, will show up to Court every time. If they don't – if they bench warrant – the Court is not going to care that it's your money. That bail is there to ensure that the person charged with the crime gets back to Court. If they don't, it gets forfeited, regardless of who posted it.

Bail Bondsmen: This is the method that most people are familiar with – it's the one that you see in movies (think Midnight Run), on TV (i.e. Dog the Bounty Hunter), etc. This is where you, or someone else, hires a bail bondsman to post bail. If you're looking for a bail bondsman, your attorney will almost always be able to provide you with the name of one. If they can't, that's a red flag that you may want to find a different attorney.

In the case of a bail bondsman, they're going to be the one to post the "bond" for you. When the judge sets bail, you'll hear him say something along the lines of "I'm setting bail in the amount of X cash, Y fully secured bond, and Z partially secured bond." In that case – Y is the amount that you will tell the bail bondsman you need to have posted.

When you reach out to the bail bondsman, they're going to want the following information:

- First of all, they're going to need to know the amount of the bond. As I said before, that's going to be the part where the judge says I'm setting bail in the amount of Y fully secured bond. If you're unsure about the amount of bail on your case, your attorney should be able to tell you.
- Once you start speaking with the bondsman, they'll let you know how much money you need to give them before they'll put up the bond. Typically, that's going to be 10% of the amount set. They'll also discuss their fee with you.
- Then, they're going to want some assurances that you are good for the money. Because they're posting the bond on your behalf, they need to know that if you end up bench warranting, they're not going to be out that money. They'll want to know

that you, or whoever is hiring them, has collateral to cover the bond.

- Collateral: The bondsman is going to be looking to make sure you are good to repay the bond if necessary. For example, they'll often ask you if you own a home, a car, or any other assets. They also may ask whether you're working, and to see your recent paystubs or tax returns.

Partially Secured Bond: Because the bail statute was revised a few years ago, there is now a third option that the judge will give you with respect to bail – this is the partially secured bond. With a partially secured bond, typically a friend or family member is essentially going to become the bail bondsman. They're going to go in front of the court, they're going to post whatever percentage of the bail the court deems necessary (usually 10% of the total amount set). Then, they are going to say to the court, "I'm going to be responsible for the bail bond if this person does not appear in court." If you do not appear in court, and the court has to issue a warrant for you, the Court will look to them to satisfy that bond. Because of that, the Court will usually make an inquiry into that person's financial ability to cover the bond.

How the Amount of Bail is Determined

The bail argument is focused on the likelihood of you returning to Court.

Your lawyer and the Assistant District Attorney are going to argue this out. The ADA may say something along the lines of, "Well, Mr. X has a bench warrant history. He's a flight risk because he has been convicted of several crimes in the past. Mr. X is not employed, and he's charged with a very serious crime that carries significant jail time."

The ADA is going to highlight every reason that you might not return to Court. Then, it's your attorney's job to explain to the Court why the ADA is wrong. It's your attorney's job to tell the Court that you're not a flight risk, to say something along the lines of, "No, no. He hasn't been convicted of any crimes – the ADA is referring to charges that were eventually dismissed. In fact, any time he has been charged with a crime in the past, he has always showed up in court. He has numerous family members seated in the audience, he has significant family and community ties. He's a lifelong resident of this county. He's employed and he owns a home. He's someone who's going to return to court. In fact, he was interviewed by pre-trial release, and they scored him very well. He is not going to be a flight risk."

Ultimately, the judge is the one who's going to make the final decision on bail or non-monetary restrictions. While there are quite a few different types of non-monetary restrictions that he may choose from, some of the more common ones include orders of protection, enrolling in some type of program or treatment, enrolling in pre-trial services or pre-trial probation, or sometimes even wearing a GPS monitoring ankle bracelet or surrendering your passport.

Are All Charges Bail Eligible Offenses?

No. Fortunately, the New York State Legislature passed a bail reform bill that modified the bail statute and at this time, not all charges are bail eligible. In fact, there are many charges that are not bail-eligible, although most of them are misdemeanors. With that being said, the D.A. can try and get around that in certain situations. Typically, that happens in situations where there are allegations of a violation of an order of protection, in domestic cases, or when someone has multiple bench warrants. Your attorney should know whether or not your offense is bail eligible, or at least be able to look it up if he doesn't know off-hand.

CHAPTER 4

WHAT HAPPENS ONCE I'M RELEASED FROM JAIL?

After the arraignment, you'll be given your next court date. You must appear in court on that next date. I've heard too many excuses from folks saying that they forgot the date, that they had to work, that they just couldn't make it – please understand, the Court does not want to hear an excuse (with one or two exceptions – typically related to illness). I'll say it again, you must appear on that next date. If you don't, some bad things are going to happen with respect to your case, and there's very little that your attorney can do. If bail was set, it may be forfeited. If bail wasn't set, they may issue a bench warrant for you, and then when you return, the judge may set bail or non-monetary conditions.

As far as your release, depending on which Court you're in, you may get some different paperwork when you walk out the door. For instance, if you did not hire an attorney for your arraignment, in Long Island, the Courts will sometimes keep the paperwork in the court file to give to whoever your attorney is on the next date - whether that be legal aid, 18-b or a private attorney. In other counties, they will have you take the paperwork yourself and then you're responsible for getting it to your attorney. If that's the case, you'll be given a copy of the criminal court complaint, a copy of the notices, and a copy of your rap sheet, which will show all your prior criminal convictions. In certain cases like DWI's, they may give you some preliminary discovery materials such as a breathalyzer report. In other cases, like domestic violence cases, you may be given an order of protection (aka a restraining order). Regardless of what paperwork you are given, it is critical that you get it to your attorney for his review.

Mistakes That People Make After Release

One question that I get asked fairly frequently, is what a person shouldn't do after they're released. Here are some common mistakes I see people make after that initial arraignment:

Not Appearing Back In Court: Probably the most common mistake that people make is not coming back to court on the next date. Honestly, I cannot stress this enough – you MUST show back up to court; if you don't, putting aside the bench warrants and the possibility of your bail getting forfeited, here's an additional list of what may happen:

- It may damage your ability to negotiate a plea deal with the ADA.
- It may hurt your credibility with the judge, and you must remember that at the end of the day, any plea deal worked out between your attorney and the DA is subject to the judge's approval.
- It will show up as a bench warrant on your rap sheet, and if you're ever arrested in the future, it will hurt your bail argument at that time.

Violating The Order Of Protection: Although not necessarily as common, I would say, an even greater mistake, is violating the order of protection that's issued by the Court. Once you violate that order of protection, a couple of things are going to happen:

- First of all, you're going to get re-arrested. This means you're going to get a new case with a criminal contempt charge. Whether that's a misdemeanor or a felony depends on the allegations against you.
- The judge is not going to be as lenient with bail. If he released you on your own recognizance on the last case, he may not do so now. If he set bail on the last case, he may set higher bail on this case.
- The violation may cause the ADA to withdraw any potential offer that your attorney has worked out, and if one has not been worked out yet, it will almost certainly put a strain on your attorney's ability to work out a resolution on your case.

With all of that being said, I'm sure your next question is what is the order of protection?

CHAPTER 5

WHAT IS AN ORDER OF PROTECTION AND WHEN IS IT ISSUED AFTER RELEASE?

The order of protection is what people commonly refer to as a restraining order. The most important thing to know is that it's a court order from the judge. If you violate it, you're blatantly disobeying the Court's order, so the judge is not going to be happy when you come back to court and he finds out.

Orders of protection come in a couple different varieties and can have different carveouts depending upon the specific circumstances. First let's talk about the order of protection itself – and keep in mind we're just limiting this to Criminal Court orders of protection. There are also Family Court orders of protection that I'm not going to discuss here. Family Court petitions for an order of protection are made in Family Court, and have a different procedure than criminal court orders. If you have any questions about them though, feel free to contact my office at any time.

At any rate, the first type of order of protection that we'll discuss is the Full Order of Protection (FOP), otherwise known as a full stay away order.

The Full Order Of Protection

The full order of protection, or full stay away order, is exactly what it sounds like – it's an order from the Court telling you to completely stay away from the other person. That means you cannot go anywhere near their home, place of employment, school, etc. It also means that you cannot have any contact with them.

This includes, no phone calls, no text messages, no e-mail, no Facebook, no Instagram, no TikTok, no Twitter, etc., it means no contact at all. It also means no third-party contact. You cannot have a third party reach out to the person on your behalf. For example, you cannot tell your mother-in-law to communicate a message to your wife if your wife has a full order of protection against you. That's considered third-party contact - it's a violation of the order – and you can be re-arrested for that.

This also means that you cannot speak with the person named in the order, even if they reach out to you. That's a question that I get from clients fairly frequently – "But Mike, my ex keeps calling me, she's texting me, she's telling me she forgives me and she doesn't want the order." Unfortunately, in those circumstances it's not up to the complainant. Once the Court has issued the full order of protection, the Court is the only one that can modify it. It does not matter if the complainant no longer wants the order. If you're in a situation where you have a full order of protection against you and the person keeps calling/texting/e-mailing/etc., the best thing to do is not answer, and to let your attorney know.

I realize this might be difficult. I realize there are a lot of emotions involved when we talk about domestic cases and orders of protection. However, it's important to realize that even though the complainant might forgive you today, they may get angry with you again tomorrow. If that happens, then all they need to do is show the police their phone records, and you'll find yourself getting rearrested.

Even if you don't think that this might happen, it's imperative that you stay away from the other person when there's a full order of protection against you. Not doing so can lead to additional charges, and the Domestic Violence Detectives often look to re-arrest people in these situations. In fact, I've witnessed this both as an ADA and as a defense attorney - the DV Detectives almost always make home visits to check in with the complainant and to see how they are doing. They're not just doing this to check on the complainant. They're also doing it to see whether you went back to the home where you are not supposed to be. The problem here is that if the officer is aware of the order and sees you in a location you're not allowed to be, he can arrest you without the other person even making a complaint. And now, even if your friend/spouse/etc., does not want to move forward with the case, the DA has a strong case against you for criminal contempt, where they only need to call the police officer as an eyewitness.

Limited Order of Protection

The second type of order typically issued in criminal cases, is the limited order of protection. Depending where you are, you might hear it called a "refrain from" order or a "do not harass" order – that's more common on Long Island. With this order, you'll still be able to be around the complainant – you just won't be allowed to commit any crimes against them. You can't attack them, you can't assault them, no criminal mischief, no harassment, etc.

You might be thinking, "Well, I can't commit any crimes against them anyway." That's true. However, the distinction here is that if you assaulted someone without the order of protection in place, you'd only be charged with assault. If there's an order of protection, you'll not only be charged with the assault, you'll also be charged with criminal contempt - and depending on the circumstances, that contempt might even elevate your case from a misdemeanor to a felony.

Additionally, if you do get arrested for criminal contempt, you're going to find that the judge is not going to be as lenient with bail, he will most likely issue a full stay away order this time, and the D.A.'s office will probably be less willing to negotiate with your lawyer.

Carveouts and Modifications

What is a carveout you ask? Well, an order of protection is not necessarily a one-size fits all type of document. Because of that, there are some modifications that we occasionally see made to orders of protection. This is typically done to accommodate people with some specific situations - and some are more common than others.

- Firearms restrictions – I would say almost every single order of protection I've ever seen has this box checked. It's applicable to both full and limited orders of protection, and essentially it says that you must surrender any and all firearms to the local precinct, and you cannot purchase any new ones while the order is in effect.
- Subject to Family Court modification – possibly the most common modification we see, is when the judge marks the order of protection subject to Family Court modification. This typically comes up in domestic situations where children are involved, and it allows the person to take the order of protection to Family Court and apply for it to be modified to accommodate things such as visitation, custody, etc.
- The Access Order – also a fairly common modification that gets made to full orders of protection – this comes up when you reside with the complainant and are now prevented from returning home as a result of the order. In this

case, the judge marks the order to allow you to return to the home with a police escort, during certain hours, to retrieve some personal property, medication, etc. It is absolutely critical you understand that this must be done **with a police escort** and if you return without a police officer, you can be rearrested. To get a cop to accompany you, you must bring the access order to the local precinct and show them the order. Understand though, it's not a license to retrieve every single item you own that's in the house – it just allows you to retrieve some necessities.

- Subject to incidental contact – we see this a little less frequently than the other two, but still commonly nonetheless - this is a modification to the full order that allows you to pass by the other party in certain common areas. We see this sometimes when folks have a dispute with a neighbor in their apartment building. The concern here is that they might run into each other on the stairs or while walking in and out of the building, so as a result, the judge marks the order "subject to incidental contact" in certain areas.

- Alcohol and drug restrictions – not particularly common, but at times when the underlying allegations involve alcohol and drugs, sometimes the judge might mark the order of protection in such a way that you're not allowed to be under the influence of alcohol or drugs while in the presence of the other party – this comes up sometimes with "endangering the welfare of a child" cases.
- The police officer firearm carveout – This one is a rare one but still comes up from time to time. When a cop is charged with a crime that results in an order of protection, they must surrender their firearms. At times, we can work out a resolution with the D.A.'s office where the officer is still able to carry his firearm while performing his official duties as a police officer. This allows him/her to go back to work.

CHAPTER 6

IMPORTANCE OF HIRING A CRIMINAL DEFENSE ATTORNEY EARLY IN THE CASE

The Pre-Arrest

Even before you've been arrested it's a good idea to consider consulting with a criminal defense attorney. If you think there may be a warrant for your arrest, or you've been contacted by the police regarding a warrant, an attorney can be very helpful. When a client approaches me at this stage of the case, it allows me to really get control of everything from early on. I'm able to speak with the Detective or Police Officer regarding the possible charges, determine whether it's a good idea to have the client give a statement, and coordinate a voluntary surrender with the police department.

I have clients come in a lot at this stage when the police officer leaves a business card at their door. Usually what happens is they leave their card with a note saying, "Hey, I want you to give me a call." It's not always specific, and it doesn't always let you know that you're under investigation for a crime. That is definitely something to remember – the police do not have to be up front and honest with you, and when it comes to apprehending you, they typically are not.

In these circumstances though, I usually try to work out a voluntary surrender with the police department. There are a few reasons that the voluntary surrender is preferable to you being arrested at home or on the street. When you voluntarily surrender, it signals to the District Attorney's Office, the Police Department, and the Court, that you're taking this seriously. You're not someone who's trying to run away. You're turning yourself in. You've hired an attorney and you're answering these charges - these allegations against you. You deny them, you're going to fight them, and you're not going to be running from them. And this is something that helps us when we make the bail argument on behalf of the client.

Another reason that the voluntary surrender is helpful, is it allows us to control the timing of when you're going into custody. I know this may not seem important, but it certainly becomes important when you don't want to spend the next forty-eight hours in a holding cell. By voluntarily surrendering, we're able to work out a time with the police officer to try and minimize the amount of time you spend in custody before seeing a judge.

Furthermore, by working out a time to voluntarily surrender, we ensure that you won't be picked up at work, at home, or randomly on the street. Being arrested in front of your family, friends, or even co-workers can be really embarrassing, and by voluntarily surrendering we're usually able to avoid that.

In addition to working out a date/time for a voluntary surrender with the police, at this stage of the case I'm also able to speak directly with the cop about the charges. This lets us get some early insight into the allegations and helps us jumpstart your defense.

It also gives us an opportunity to see whether we can get the detective to issue you a desk appearance ticket instead of taking you into custody. A desk appearance ticket is essentially a summons to come back to court, and although not everyone is eligible for one, we do always try to speak with the Detective about it.

Finally, probably the most important reason to get my firm involved with your case early on, is it allows us to let the Detective know that you are represented by counsel and you should not be interrogated. This prevents them from questioning you about the case.

It Is Absolutely Essential That You Be Honest And Up Front At The Initial Consultation

The Importance Of Honesty: At our initial consultation, honesty is absolutely critical. We'll be speaking about many different topics, including what happened, what the underlying facts are, and also about your background. Each of these topics is essential to discuss as it's important that I have a full understanding of your case. Complete honesty at this stage is so critical because withholding important information at the beginning only leads to significant difficulties throughout the case.

First and foremost, at this stage I will be speaking with the Police Department and District Attorney's Office about your case. This will include discussing your background. I handle my clients with a holistic approach, and knowing all about your background allows me to approach the District Attorney's Office with this information so that they can see you as a person, not just another file on their desk.

With that being said, the information I go to them with, must be accurate and true. If I approach them with false information and they feel that we are trying to deceive them, this may irreparably damage our credibility with them for the rest of the case. Then it becomes much more difficult when I attempt to negotiate a favorable resolution to your case.

Secondly, I need to know exactly what happened. The beginning of a case can be critical in terms of our investigation into the case. Knowing all of the important information up front lets me know how we need to attack the case. Do we want to hire a private investigator? Do they need to be sent out right away? Do we need to ask that the D.A. preserve specific evidence? These are all questions that come up at the beginning of the case, and if you do not provide me with the proper information, we might end up with the wrong answers. While you may think that we can always talk about these things later, the fact is that surveillance video can be deleted within days of an incident, witnesses might disappear, and other pieces of critical evidence can be lost if we don't act quickly. Because of that, it's absolutely essential for me to know all of the facts up front.

How Often Will I Have Court Appearances And Will I Need To Attend Them In-Person?

How often you'll have Court Appearances is going to depend largely on whether you're charged with a felony or a misdemeanor, and whether you are incarcerated or out on bail. Typically, felony cases will be adjourned for roughly two (2) to four (4) weeks, and misdemeanor cases are usually adjourned about thirty (30) days or more. With that being said, this is more an estimate than a rule, because ultimately it all comes down to the Court's schedule.

As far as whether you'll have to appear in-person, at the courthouse – that's going to depend on the county that you've been arrested in. At this point, the Courts have shifted back to almost 100% in-person appearances, with some exceptions for emergency medical situations. However, some courts will occasionally allow your attorney to appear without you being present. This typically happens in situations where the case is just on for conference and there is no expectation that a plea, hearing, or trial is going to occur. Additionally, in some lower-level offense cases (traffic tickets and summonses), the Courts may allow your attorney to appear on your behalf without you being present, as long as he has a signed authorization to do so.

With that being said, you should absolutely always show up to Court unless your attorney explicitly tells you not to – let me repeat that, you MUST show up to court, unless you are explicitly told not to. If you don't, you'll end up getting a bench warrant for your arrest, and as I've discussed earlier – you don't want that.

CHAPTER 7

IS THERE ANYTHING THAT I SHOULD BE DOING IN-BETWEEN MY COURT DATES THAT COULD HELP MY DEFENSE?

Keep In Contact With Your Attorney

The most important thing is to keep in contact with your attorney and return their calls when they call you. When I call my clients, it's because I need information on your case, and more likely than not, it's something important. I may need an important piece of information for negotiation purposes, I may need you to do something, I may have an update for you – there are any number of reasons that your attorney may be reaching out to you, but I can tell you from experience, they're not just reaching out to shoot the breeze. So please, be sure to call your attorney back as soon as possible.

Additionally, if you don't hear from your attorney for a while, you should try reaching out to them. While I do my best to keep in contact with my clients in-between court dates, I can't speak for other lawyers. Oftentimes this case is going to be one of the most important things in your lives, and if you don't hear from your lawyer, reach out to them for an update. No attorney is going to be unhappy (or at least they should not be unhappy) with you reaching out to them for a status update on your case.

Do Your Homework

I know, hearing that you have homework probably brings back some bad childhood memories – but trust me, if your attorney gives you "homework" to do, make sure you do it. What do I mean by homework? Anything that your lawyer asks you to do in between court dates. For my clients, there's usually two (2) things I ask them to do on almost every case.

Getting Evaluated For a Treatment Program

When a case calls for it, I always ask my clients to voluntarily get evaluated for possible treatment. The fact of the matter is, our society has become far more enlightened in recent years, and rather than simply relying upon punitive justice, many D.A.'s are open to restorative justice – in other words, treatment.

What do I mean by treatment? Well, that will depend on the facts of your case. For instance, if you have an alcohol-related case (think DWI, bar fight, etc.) then I will typically be advising the client that it's a good idea to get evaluated by a licensed and certified alcohol treatment provider, and, if the evaluation comes back that they need treatment, I'll generally recommend that they enroll in it. This does not stop at alcohol cases - it extends to drug treatment, anger management, defensive driving, psychosexual treatment, mental treatment, and many other types of treatment and counseling depending on the situation.

Why should you voluntarily get evaluated and enroll in the treatment program? Because when we talk about resolving a criminal case at the negotiation table rather than in the courtroom, many A.D.A's tend to be far more willing to sit down and negotiate when they see that the person is taking their case seriously. Getting evaluated for treatment shows them that you are taking it seriously, that you are remorseful for what you did, and that you are looking to fix the mistake. As a former prosecutor, I can tell you that A.D.A's often prefer to resolve a case with rehabilitative justice where you complete counseling and treatment, rather than just blindly pursuing jail time on a case.

Character Reference Letters

Another form of homework I give my clients is to gather character reference letters from friends, family, and colleagues. This becomes important because most A.D.A.'s are typically handling hundreds (no exaggeration there) of cases at a time. They walk in every morning to a new stack of files sitting on their desk. It becomes easy for them to just push the files through, and to treat each person as just another folder on their desk.

We don't want that. What we want is for the A.D.A. to see that you stand out from that stack of files. The way that I do that, is I typically submit a pre-pleading memorandum on each of my cases where I utilize my interviews with you, the character reference letters that you provide me with, and any other information that you give me, to illustrate all of the things that will make you stand out from every other folder on the A.D.A.'s desk.

By doing this, I remind the A.D.A. that my client is someone who has a family – a spouse, kids, etc., -

people who depend on him/her. I remind them that these "folders" on their desk, are mothers, fathers, brothers, sisters - usually folks who are otherwise good people, contributing members of society, that may have just made a mistake.

By humanizing you to the Assistant District Attorney, we're able to get them to consider more reasonable resolutions to your case that are more favorable to you.

If I Have Any Prior Arrests Or Convictions, How Much Is That Going To Play Into My Case?

Past arrests are going to come into play on your case at multiple levels. First, going back to the arraignment, prior arrests, convictions, bench warrants, etc., are going to have an impact on the D.A.'s bail recommendation and the judge's decision on whether to set bail. If you have a string of criminal convictions and bench warrants, the judge is going to be far more inclined to set bail on you. Alternatively, if you've never been arrested before in your entire life, then there's a fairly good chance that the judge will either release you on your own recognizance, or put you on pre-trial monitoring if the charge is more serious.

Prior arrests are also going to come up at the negotiation table. The Assistant District Attorney is going to look more favorably on someone who's never been arrested before and is just being accused of having made this one mistake. Alternatively, if you've got multiple priors, the A.D.A. may be less inclined to offer a favorable plea agreement on your case.

The Effect of Felony Convictions

Any criminal conviction is serious – but a prior felony conviction is going to have the largest impact on your new case, particularly if it's a conviction within the past ten (10) years. In New York State, if you have a prior felony conviction from the past ten (10) years, you are considered a predicate felon for sentencing purposes.

Violent vs. Non-Violent Predicate Felons

First of all, let me explain what a predicate felon is – when we say someone is a predicate felon, what we mean is that they have a prior felony conviction (whether it's violent or non-violent) within the past ten (10) years, excluding any time they served in jail/prison. This becomes important, because it's going to have a huge impact on the time they may be facing on a new felony charge.

In New York State, there are statutory sentencing guidelines that judges MUST adhere to. These include a minimum and maximum amount of time that a person can be sentenced to on each felony offense. When we talk about predicate felons, these statutory minimums and maximums can increase dramatically. For instance, if you are not a predicate felon and you are charged with possessing a loaded firearm with the intent to use it unlawfully against another, your minimum sentencing time if convicted, is 3 ½ years. If you are a "violent predicate" and convicted of the same crime, your minimum sentencing time automatically goes up to 7 years – double the amount of time.

As you can see, it makes a significant difference. Additionally, if you find yourself being classified as a "mandatory persistent violent felony offender" – or someone who has two (2) separate prior violent felony convictions within the previous ten (10) years, your minimum on that gun conviction jumps right up to sixteen (16) years. There are other classifications, such as discretionary persistent felony offenders, but that is certainly something your attorney will speak with you in detail about before you take any type of plea, or go to trial.

As far as the distinction between violent and non-violent predicates, it's fairly self-explanatory. Basically, some crimes in N.Y. are classified as violent felonies, others as non-violent felonies – depending which you are convicted of dictates whether you're a violent or non-violent predicate. With all of that being said, it is absolutely essential that you speak with your attorney about these factors before taking any felony plea.

Chapter 8

Factors That Help You Decide Whether Or Not To Accept A Plea Deal

The plea deal - something that everyone has heard of. In almost every criminal case, at some point, your attorney will come to you and tell you that they've spoken with the Assistant District Attorney, and they've worked out a potential plea offer. Sometimes it will be a great offer where you walk away without a criminal conviction, and with minimal consequences. Other times, particularly in very serious cases, it may be a situation where your attorney is attempting to mitigate the amount of jail time you are looking at. Understand, ultimately it is always the client's decision whether or not to take a plea deal – I tell every single one of my clients the same thing – this is your case, this is your life, this is your decision. I can advise you on the potential consequences, but I can never decide whether or not my client should enter into a plea agreement. It's their choice.

When I speak with a client regarding a potential plea deal, we usually discuss some of these factors:

- What is the strength of the DA's case?
- What is the strength of the DA's evidence?
- Do we think that we have a case that we're going to be able to fight at trial?
- How is it going to look in front of the jury or the judge?
- Is it a case that we're likely to win at trial?
- Is it likely that the D.A. will be able to get their witnesses in for the trial? Is the complainant on the case cooperative or uncooperative?

- In a situation where the plea offer involves treatment or probation, is it going to be a good fit for the client? While treatment can oftentimes be a beneficial way to resolve a case, we certainly don't want to set you up to fail if it's a situation where you might not be able to successfully complete a program.
- What is the client's min/max exposure if we lose at trial?

And the reason that I speak with each client about these factors, is because I want to make sure that they know the best case and worst case scenarios.

What Do Plea Offers Generally Look Like For First Time Or Second Time Offenders?

This is something that's going to be very case specific. Ultimately, the allegations against you are going to be the most important factor in what we're able to work out with the A.D.A. Some other important factors are going to be the severity of the charge (is it a misdemeanor or felony offense), whether anyone was severely injured, whether there was significant property damage, etc.

For instance, if you are only charged with a misdemeanor or a violation, and it's your first offense, we've usually got a pretty good shot at walking away with a non-criminal disposition. A non-criminal disposition is a resolution to your case that does not leave you with the stigma of having a criminal conviction on your record. One common way that we can do this is with a plea to disorderly conduct (that you were acting disorderly) – which is a violation, not a crime. Sometimes, we may even be able to work out an adjournment in contemplation of dismissal – otherwise known as an ACD. An ACD is when your case gets adjourned (six months on a non-family case, one year on a family case) for a period of time, and as long as you stay out of trouble, it ultimately gets dismissed and sealed. While it's technically still an open case, as long as you abide by the conditions set by the Court (oftentimes an order of protection or community service), you ultimately end up with a dismissal. On the other hand, if you do not abide by the conditions, or you get rearrested, the D.A. can restore your case to the calendar and continue prosecuting you. While an ACD is almost always a favorable resolution to a case, it's still important to discuss it fully with your attorney before accepting it.

Another common way that we're able to resolve cases, is with a conditional plea, or an interim probation plea. When we talk about a conditional plea, the best way to think about it is the D.A. and the Court are giving you an opportunity to prove that you learned your lesson. If you do that, then you can walk away with a lesser charge, or sometimes even an outright dismissal of your case. Effectively, what happens is you plead up front to the charge against you, you do some type of treatment, probation, community service, counseling, etc., and as long as you are successful and abide by all of the conditions set by the Court, you are allowed to come back and vacate your plea. Then, after that plea is vacated, the Court resentences you to the sentence that you agreed upon at the time you took your conditional plea.

A perfect example of this happens with DWI pleas. A fairly common misdemeanor DWI plea is where you plead up front to the misdemeanor DWI charge along with the DWAI charge. You agree to do alcohol treatment, install an ignition interlock device on your vehicle, and abide by other potential conditions set by the court (i.e. use a portable breath device or an ankle bracelet that monitors whether you consume alcohol). As long as you adhere to the conditions and complete all the requirements successfully, the Court lets you come back and vacate the plea to the misdemeanor, and then it resentences you on the violation, allowing you to avoid having that misdemeanor on your record.

We see these types of pleas happen on both misdemeanor and felony cases, and even though they are excellent opportunities, they should be taken with the understanding that they oftentimes come with conditions for failure as well. For instance, many times a conditional plea comes with a jail alternative – meaning that if you fail the conditions that you agreed to, the judge will sentence you to the charge that you initially pled to, and put you in jail. Any plea should only be taken after careful consideration and discussion with your attorney.

Finally, while most of the time we are able to work out fairly favorable resolutions for first time offenses, it is important to understand that if you are charged with a very serious allegation (i.e. gun charges, serious assaults, homicide, etc.), even if it is your first offense, your attorney may not be able to work out a non-jail resolution to your case. In those circumstances, it may be more of a matter of attempting to mitigate the amount of time spent in jail. Always remember that if you're not happy with the offer on your case, you still have the right to take the case to trial.

CHAPTER 9

DO MOST CRIMINAL CASES END UP GOING TO TRIAL?

No, most cases do not go to trial. That's the simple answer.

While I don't have actual statistics, I can tell you that a very minimal amount of cases actually ends up going to trial. Instead, most cases are resolved with a negotiated plea agreement.

My initial conversation with every single one of my clients is that this is their case, it's their life, and ultimately, they must make the big decisions. They are the ones who have to live with the ramifications of the decision, and while an attorney can advise a client on the cost/benefits of taking a plea vs. taking the case to trial, the attorney should never pressure a client into a decision. If my client tells me, "Look, I know that you've worked out a great deal, and I appreciate it. But you know what, I don't think it's good enough, I want to take this to trial because I didn't do anything wrong," - then that's what we do.

If My Case Is Ultimately Dismissed Or The Charges Are Reduced, Is That The End Of It? What Is Going To Show On My Record, How Do You See People's Lives Go On After The Case?

This all depends on how the case was resolved – was it resolved with a dismissal? Was it resolved with a plea to a misdemeanor? Was it resolved with a violation? This is what's going to dictate what happens next.

For instance, if you get a disorderly conduct violation, that's going to be something that in most cases will seal. What I mean when I say it will seal, is that it will not show up in a public records search. However, that violation will still show up in a law enforcement database – so, if you're ever rearrested, the police department is going to see that. It'll also come up if you apply for a firearm, and in certain other circumstances.

What about that ACD we talked about before? Well, that's another circumstance where your case will eventually be sealed – except in that circumstance it will show up as having been dismissed and sealed. With that being said, the arrest will still be accessible to law enforcement if you're rearrested, or if you apply for a gun. But for public purposes, when it's dismissed and sealed, it should not be available to the public eye – and if you're asked if you were ever convicted of a crime, the answer is unequivocally no.

Finally, if the charges were reduced to a misdemeanor from a felony, or even to certain types of violations (i.e. PL § 240.26), they will not seal. They will appear on your record and will remain with you. Because of that, I again reiterate – talk to your attorney before you enter any type of plea.

If I Am Convicted Of A Criminal Offense, When Does The Sentencing Generally Take Place?

The sentencing is typically going to be a couple of weeks after the conviction – the Court is going to adjourn the case for what's called "interview and sentence," or a "pre-sentence investigation report." This essentially means that you'll be interviewed by probation. The judge will review the results of the probation report before sentencing you. Because the probation report can influence sentencing, it's important that you discuss the probation interview process with your attorney, so you know what to expect. The most important thing though, is that you be honest in the interview. As far as the timing, that's usually going to be somewhere along the lines of a couple of weeks, depending on whether you're in or out of custody.

Sometimes in certain circumstances, such as if you pled guilty to a violation or even a misdemeanor, this requirement may be waived, and the judge may sentence you on the spot.

What Does The Judge Consider When Looking At A Sentence Or Determining A Sentence?

The judge is going to consider multiple factors when they decide on the sentence. First and foremost, they're going to consider whether it was a negotiated plea and whether there is a negotiated sentence. However, even in those circumstances, they're still going to look at that probation report. What's going to be in that report is all of this background information on you - where you live, where you work, whether you have substance abuse problems, and whether you accept responsibility for what you pled guilty to. I'll say it again - you must talk about that interview with your attorney because there are certain things that you absolutely must do in that interview.

You must be honest with probation. For instance, if you pled guilty to a crime, and then lie during the probation interview, telling them you didn't actually commit the crime, that's going to cause a problem at sentencing. When you take a plea, you do so under oath. Therefore, if you tell probation later that you did not in fact commit that crime, the Court will either assume you are lying to probation, or view your plea as perjury, and when the judge sees this, he is not going to be happy.

In addition to that probation report, the judge is also going to consider any arguments from the District Attorney's Office as well as any arguments that your attorney may make on your behalf. In most cases where there is a negotiated plea, the A.D.A. and your attorney are both going to simply rely upon the sentence that was promised to you at the time of plea. However, in certain circumstances, this may not be the case.

What might happen instead, is the District Attorney's Office may submit victim impact letters, which are going to be letters from the victim of the crime. For instance, in a homicide, you would see letters coming from the family talking about how the loss of this person has impacted them, how angry they are or how sad they are – how difficult their life has become as a result of the crime. The judge may give them an opportunity to read the letters or even to speak, and that'll all be done at the sentencing. Additionally, your attorney will be able to present information on your behalf, and you will even have an opportunity to speak at sentencing yourself, should you choose to do so.

Is There Anything That I Can Or Should Do Before The Sentencing Hearing That Could Help The Outcome Of My Case?

The most important thing is going to be speaking with your attorney and making sure that you're well prepared for that probation interview. Your attorney should be able to help you prepare for both the probation interview and sentencing hearing. If there is information that you want to present at sentencing, you should bring it to your attorney's attention so that you can go over it together and discuss the best way to move forward. It's also going to be imperative that you do not get rearrested between your conviction and your sentencing date. If you get rearrested, the judge does not have to adhere to any promised sentence that they may have made when you entered the plea, and while you may have pled guilty with the thought of getting the minimum sentence, you may find yourself facing the maximum instead.

If Probation Is Part Of My Sentence, What Sort Of Things Are Important To Know About This Part Of The Criminal Justice System?

The important thing to know about probation is that you must strictly abide by their conditions. Probation is not always easy to deal with. Once you're sentenced to probation, you're going to have to sign up with them immediately. They'll generally put some requirements in place to monitor you and ensure you do not reoffend. This will depend on your case – it will depend on the severity of the case, the recommendation of the D.A., whether there were any treatment conditions that were part of your plea, etc. For instance, a component of your probation may be to do a sex offender treatment program, an alcohol treatment program, or even community service. There are any number of conditions that probation can impose upon you as part of your release, but it is absolutely essential that you abide by them.

You will also have to check in with your probation officer on a specific date/time. Your P.O. will always let you know how frequently this must be done. Sometimes this may mean that you only have to check in with them a couple of times a month. If you were charged with a more serious crime and they want to keep a close tab on you, then that may not be the case. But ultimately, the most important thing is that you abide by the conditions that probation sets. The probation officer is going to be the one who can attempt to violate your probation, and if they do, you can potentially be looking at doing jail time on the case.

When I'm Sentenced, Are There Alternatives To Jail?

Sometimes. I've already discussed a few of these – but typically when we talk about sentencing, you're looking at a few different options. The first, of course, is jail time. Then there's probation. There's also a "conditional discharge" which is like probation in that you agree to abide by certain conditions, but you're not actually being strictly monitored. However, if you violate the CD you can end up in jail the same way as if you violated probation.

In addition to these commonly known sentences, there are some that people are not as familiar with. These are typically referred to as "alternative sentencing programs" or "diversion programs." Effectively, they're treatment programs where the Court allows you to plead guilty and enter into them as part of your plea.

We spoke earlier about conditional pleas, but these are a bit different because they're usually monitored directly by court personnel rather than the treatment provider and the D.A.'s office. One example is Drug Diversion Court. To enter Drug Diversion Court, you generally plea upfront, and then you enter the program. In fact, some jurisdictions will even let you enter the program without pleading up front and engage in "no-plea diversion." This isn't all that common, but it does sometimes happen when we have to deal with certain types of collateral consequences that could stem from an upfront plea.

After the plea (or no-plea), you typically have to a do the program. As long as you're successful with all of the conditions set by the Court, and you complete the program successfully, you usually end up getting to take your plea back and getting a much better offer.

Sometimes that's a misdemeanor down from a felony or in certain circumstances it can result in a violation or even a full dismissal.

Now, in addition to drug diversion court, some of the courts also have programs for young people who are first-time offenders with a first-time firearm charge. You have to qualify for it, but if you are accepted into it, it allows you to participate in a program rather than ending up in jail.

There's also mental health treatment court, veterans court, alcohol diversion, and many other types of treatment courts that are available. The bottom line is that even if you are charged with a crime, there are options out there, especially for first-time offenders. Speak with your attorney about these things and he will advocate on your behalf to try and work out the best possible resolution on your case.

Is It A Good Idea To Just Go Ahead And Plead Guilty Right From The Start?

No, you almost never want to just plead guilty at the first court appearance.

While it's natural to want to get your case resolved quickly, you must understand the severity of the charges against you. Whether it's a felony, a misdemeanor, or even a violation, each can have significant collateral consequences on a person's life. A plea can potentially impact your job, your financial aid if you're in college, your ability to get into college, your immigration status, or even your ability to apply for public assistance.

A criminal conviction is something that is going to follow you for the rest of your life. Because of that, it is never a good idea to just say, "I don't have the time for this. I'm just going to plead guilty," without at least trying to resolve the case.

If, after speaking with your attorney, you want to just plead guilty to the top count, you can always do that later. It serves your interests much better to at least attempt to negotiate with the D.A., to look at the facts, look at the evidence, see what's appropriate in the case, and see whether it's a case that you should fight at trial. This is your life that you're dealing with, and it's never a good idea to just lose hope and give up.

I tell every single one of my clients to never give up – even if they seem to have lost hope – That's what we're here for – to fight for you when you have no fight left in you.

CHAPTER 10

WHAT TO LOOK FOR WHEN SEARCHING FOR A CRIMINAL DEFENSE ATTORNEY?

Knowledgeable

You want someone knowledgeable about criminal defense. You want someone who is going to be able to speak about everything that I've mentioned above. If the criminal defense lawyer you speak to can't touch on each of these subjects, then they're not the person that you want representing you. Remember, this is your life on the line.

Dedication

You also want to ensure that you choose an attorney who is going to be dedicated to your case. The number one complaint I get from people that hire me after firing their previous lawyer, is that their previous lawyer did not give them the time and attention that they deserved.

This is your life. Odds are this case is going to be one of the most important things to happen to you throughout your entire life. Choose an attorney that will give you the time that you not only need, but that you deserve. A good lawyer will listen to everything that you have to tell them and stay on top of your case. He will keep you updated, answer your questions, return your calls, and ensure that he fights for you every step of the way.

Prosecutorial Experience

If I were hiring an attorney to represent me on a criminal case, I'd want one with prosecutorial experience – someone who has worked at the D.A.'s office. That's someone who is going to know who they are fighting against. They're going to know the players, and they're going to know how to resolve your case.

They're going to know what the D.A. is looking for and how to negotiate with the prosecutor to ensure that you get the best possible resolution on your case. They'll also know what to do when a deal can't be worked out.

Finally, you also want someone who's going to fight for your rights, who is going to fight for the best possible resolution, and who's going to fight for you at trial. At the end of the day, you don't want someone who is a push over – you want an attorney who fights!

Should I Even Hire A Lawyer? What Can I Expect When Hiring Mike Schillinger To Defend Me?

You can expect that I'm going to fight like hell for you.

Look, could you represent yourself in a criminal case? You might be able to; some people can. They're able to investigate the law and get an idea of what they're supposed to be doing. But at the end of the day, it's never a good idea to represent yourself on a case.

Your attorney is going to be able to say things in court that you simply cannot. They're going to be able to speak on the record and say things that if you said, you might find the D.A. using against you later on. They'll be able to negotiate with the District Attorney's Office without having the fear that the court reporter or the D.A. will use it at trial.

Furthermore, when I get a case, I know the proper way to negotiate it - what the typical plea offers are going to be, and how to talk to the A.D.A. I can look at the evidence with an eye that an average person simply does not have – it's a trait that comes from experience – from working on these types of cases for years. The same way that you would go to a Dentist to pull your tooth - Could you pull your own tooth? Probably. But is it a good idea? No. Criminal cases can have significant impacts on people's lives, and hiring an experienced lawyer to represent you is the only way to ensure that you minimize the potential impacts. When we talk about criminal cases, it's your liberty that's at stake – your freedom.

What Sets You Apart As A Criminal Defense Attorney In New York State?

You will have direct contact with me every step of the way.

I give every single one of my clients my office number and my personal cell phone number. I answer my phone 24 hours a day, 7 days a week. If for some reason I'm not able to answer the phone, you'll be speaking with someone from my staff who will always be able to get in contact with me one way or the other. If I'm in court or otherwise unable to answer, I make sure to call every single client back as soon as possible, and always within twelve (12) to twenty-four (24) hours.

Experience

In addition to being accessible to my clients, I also have a wealth of experience handling criminal cases on both sides. I've worked as an Assistant District

Attorney, I've been on the other side. I know how to speak to the prosecutors and how to negotiate the best possible resolution. I also know what to do when negotiating doesn't work. Having worked in the D.A.'s office, I know how they handle their cases and what to look for when we bring the fight to the courtroom.

In addition to knowing how to fight inside and outside of the courtroom, I also have something most defense attorneys don't have – the compassion that my clients deserve. Having worked for a member of Congress for over eight (8) years, I understand when you walk into the office that this is going to be the most difficult thing that you're probably going to go through in your life. The unfortunate truth of it is I constantly get new clients that tell me how their previous attorney did not give them the time of day, that they weren't approachable, and that they did not treat them with the compassion that they thought they deserved. I've been working for people who are experiencing tragedies in their lives for my entire career, even before I became a lawyer. I've worked in both the public and private sector, and have helped countless people through tragedies – Every single case that I take on, every single client that I agree to help, is treated with the compassion and care that they deserve.

I have the passion, compassion, and empathy that you need. I also understand that the holistic approach to my clients is the best way to get the best resolution at the negotiation table, and that when all else fails, we bring the fight to the court room.

Experience, Drive, & Fight

In addition to my experience at the negotiation table, I also have the experience, the drive, and the ability to fight for my clients at trial. I know the importance of taking the fight to the courtroom, and doing everything I can to advocate on your behalf.

I ensure that each of my clients has someone pushing for them every step of the way – from the arraignment all the way to trial, I fight like hell for every single person that asks me to stand in their corner.

What Is The Next Step?

I know that there's a lot of information in this book and I'm sure you must have additional questions about your case or the criminal justice system in general. I welcome the opportunity to speak with anyone who has read my book and has additional follow-up questions.

My office number is (631) 650-6900 and the phones are answered 24/7. Additionally, if you prefer to contact me by e-mail, I can be reached at contact@michaelschillinger.com. If you have any questions at all, or just want to chat with someone about your case and what options you might have, please don't hesitate to contact me at any time.

I hope all of this information was helpful!

- Mike

INDEX

Notes

Made in United States
North Haven, CT
13 April 2024

51290294R00062